DATE		
OCT 9		
OCT 23		
JAN		
FEB 14		
Forl.		

WHY DO WARS HAPPEN ?

© Aladdin Books 1988

Designed and produced by
Aladdin Books Ltd, 70 Old Compton Street, London W1V 5PA

Editor: Catherine Bradley
Design: Rob Hillier
Research: Cecilia Weston-Baker
Illustration: Ron Hayward Associates
Consultant: Angela Grunsell

Don Slater is a lecturer in sociology and
communications at Goldsmith's College, London.

Angela Grunsell is an advisory teacher specializing in
development education and resources for the primary
school age range.

Published in the United States in 1988 by
Gloucester Press, 387 Park Avenue South, New York, NY10016

ISBN 0 531 17114 0

Library of Congress Catalog
Card Number: 88 50514

Printed in Belgium

"LET'S TALK ABOUT"

WHY DO WARS HAPPEN ?

DON SLATER

Gloucester Press
New York · London · Toronto · Sydney

"What is a war?"

Sometimes when you are watching TV you may see pictures about war. Have you ever felt so angry you wanted to hit someone? A war is different from a violent argument between two people. It is a violent argument between two countries or between groups of people who live in the same country. Wars are fought by soldiers, airmen and sailors.

Wars are fought for many reasons. This book will help you understand some of them.

4

On TV you may see news about real wars and also made up stories about war.

Young children may get into fights. But there are other ways to sort out differences.

"Why do people fight?"

You may get into arguments at school and feel so angry or upset that you fight. You might have something someone else wants. You may feel that is the only way to protect yourself or someone else. You can try to sort it out by talking or calling in a teacher. You do not have to fight.

When countries or groups of people go to war, it is often because they feel they have no other choice. They may regret the violence but see it as the only way to achieve their aims.

"Who fights in a war?"

It is mostly men who plan and fight wars. Perhaps this is because of the different ways in which girls and boys are brought up. While grown-ups expect girls to play peaceful games, they often encourage boys to play with guns and be rough.

Boys are also taught that it is good to be strong and that they should test their strength. Many games are about beating other people at all costs in order to win. Sometimes older boys join gangs that fight each other.

8

By pretending to be soldiers, boys sometimes come to believe that war is exciting. They may also feel they must fight to show that they are brave and strong.

Wars are fought by armies not individual people. Armies are made up of soldiers trained to obey orders and to kill other people. Soldiers, airmen and sailors often see fighting as just another job. But being in a war can be very frightening. People may be killed or badly hurt. Sometimes soldiers refuse to obey orders.

Many people decide to join an army because they believe a war is right. They believe that the government, or those who began the war, are doing the best thing to protect them.

Most armies today are made up of men who see fighting as their job. In times of war more people are called up to join the army. Some may agree with the war but some may disagree and not want to fight.

There is a danger that war may sometimes seem like a video game: you just destroy blips on the screen and the enemy is wiped out. Some soldiers find it very hard to do what is expected of them.

"How do we create enemies?"

Soldier are taught and trained so that they do not see the enemy as real people. "They are not like us." Soldiers often fight at a distance with missiles or bombs and they do not see the people that they are killing. Perhaps this makes killing other people seem easy.

Governments may use propaganda during wartime. This is when they use TV, newspapers and the radio to show people how the enemy is wrong and they are totally right.

"What are the causes of war?"

There are many reasons why countries may go to war. Sometimes there may be a good reason for fighting other times not. Wars sometimes happen because one country wants to gain more land or territory. Sometimes a powerful country may take over a weaker one. The defeated country is occupied and used by the invaders for their own benefits. If a powerful country occupies several others they may form an empire. Until 1776, the United States was part of Britain's empire.

BE

FRAN

MOROCCO

ALGERIA

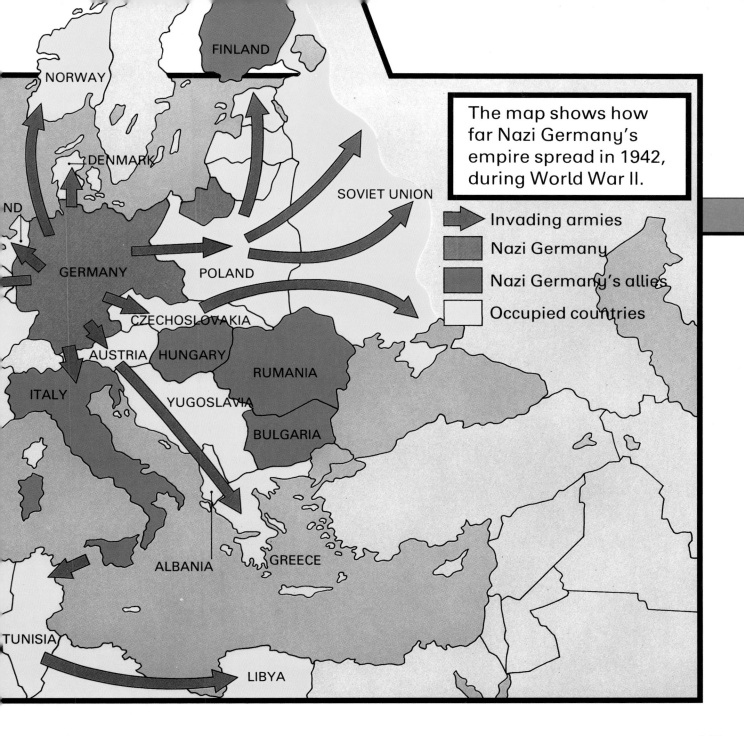

NORWAY

FINLAND

DENMARK

ND

GERMANY

POLAND

SOVIET UNION

CZECHOSLOVAKIA

AUSTRIA HUNGARY

RUMANIA

ITALY

YUGOSLAVIA

BULGARIA

ALBANIA GREECE

TUNISIA

LIBYA

The map shows how far Nazi Germany's empire spread in 1942, during World War II.

→ Invading armies

▮ Nazi Germany

▮ Nazi Germany's allies

▯ Occupied countries

Although World War II ended in 1945 there have been many smaller wars since then. Several of these occurred when countries that had been part of an empire decided to fight so that they could regain their freedom. People who have power do not usually give it up without a struggle.

For example, in Africa Angola fought a long war to free itself from rule by Portugal. It won its independence in 1975. But now Angola's powerful neighbor, South Africa, is backing a rebel group so there is a civil war – a war within a country.

Different groups in Angola are fighting for power. Even children feel that they have a part to play in this war.

Countries sometimes fight over resources: to gain good farmland, rich mines or a seaport for their ships to use. Countries may also argue about their borders and claim that some of their neighbor's territory rightfully belongs to them.

Some people go to war because of different ideas about how to live. The Gulf War between Iran and Iraq started as a war over territory but there were other reasons, mainly religious differences. Now they are fighting to prove that they are the most powerful country in the region.

Iran is fighting a "holy" war against Iraq: men, women and boys get military training.

"Who suffers in a war?"

There have been two "total wars" this century, involving many countries and powerful weapons. Civilians — people not in the army — may be killed, wounded or forced to leave their homes. They may become refugees, or may suffer starvation and ill health because armies take away their food and land. Cities are destroyed. Everyone suffers.

London in flames in 1940. During World War II over 40 million people died.

SMITHS'

FLOORS
TO be LET
FARMER&SONS

ADVERTISING AGENCY

PUBLICITY HOUSE

SHAVING

PUNCH
TAVERN

21

Some FB-111 jet fighters at an air base. They are some of the United States' arms.

"Can we stop wars by getting rid of weapons?"

Has anyone ever threatened to bring in their Dad to win an argument? Most countries feel that as long as their enemies have arms, they will need weapons to defend themselves. This becomes an arms race, when competing countries feel they have to produce more arms than each other. The arms race between the two "superpowers" — the United States and the Soviet Union — has led both countries to spend much of their wealth on making arms. The arms industries have become powerful.

23

"What about nuclear war?"

At the end of World War II, the United States used a terrifying new weapon: the nuclear bomb. Just one bomb can destroy a city and produce deadly radiation that kills people for many years afterwards. The United States and the Soviet Union have many nuclear weapons. None of them have been used. Many people feel these weapons make war too dangerous.

A nuclear bomb is tested in the South Pacific. The United States, Soviet Union, China, India, Britain, France and Israel have nuclear bombs.

The United Nations has sent troops into Lebanon to help keep warring armies apart.

"Can wars be stopped?"

The fear of nuclear war and the great cost of the arms race have led many countries to try to prevent wars. Since World War II, some 159 countries have joined together in the United Nations. It exists to allow members to sort out problems through discussion and it sends in peace-keeping troops to stop conflicts happening.

The symbol of the United Nations. As well as trying to keep peace, it has many organizations to deal with world problems.

Millions of people in Europe and the United States have demonstrated against nuclear weapons since World War II.

Many people are working hard to stop wars. People have protested against particular wars and helped bring them to an end. For example, Americans successfully protested against their country fighting in the Vietnam War during the 1960s and 1970s. People have also demonstrated against nuclear weapons. They argue that the factories that make weapons could produce more useful things.

The superpowers have been discussing ways to halt the arms race. In December 1987 the superpower leaders signed a treaty that agreed to get rid of a small number of nuclear missiles. Getting rid of all the nuclear weapons is still a long way off, although this is a hopeful sign.

"What can I do?"

You could find out more about particular wars in the world today and who is involved in them. You could also find out about individuals and organizations that are concerned about peace. Some of the organizations listed below may be able to give information to you or your teacher for further work.

You could even write to the superpower leaders and tell them how you feel about war.

Addresses for more information

Nuclear Freeze Campaign of the 15th Congressional District
351 East 74th Street
New York, New York 10021

World Policy Institute
777 United Nations Plaza
New York, New York 10017

International Research Council
126 Alexander Street
Princeton, New Jersey 08540

What the words mean

arms race: when two countries build up stores of weapons because they don't want the other to become more powerful.

army: a group of men (or women) armed to take part in a war.

nuclear bomb: an extremely powerful weapon which uses the power released by splitting a nucleus (part of an atom).

radiation: damaging rays sent out by a nuclear bomb. Also found in X-rays and in other sources.

superpower: a very powerful country that has influence on world events.

Index

Photographic Credits:
Cover and page 22: Frank Spooner Agency; pages 4-5, 6 and 12: Sally and Richard Greenhill; pages 5 (inset), 9, 11, 18 and 26: Rex Features; page 16: Hutchison Library; page 21: IWM; page 25: USAF.

PRINTED IN BELGIUM BY
proost
INTERNATIONAL BOOK PRODUCTION